Year of the Hare

Teresa Mei Chuc

Year of the Hare

ISBN 978-0-9853151-5-3

Cover photo: Teresa Mei Chuc and her brother in Saigon, Vietnam in 1978.

Published by
Shabda Press
Post Office Box 70483
Pasadena, CA 91117

Contents

A Fetus

It was 1975, the Year of the Hare, in Saigon, Vietnam. I was a fetus the size of a half-dollar in Mama's womb, gulping down amniotic fluid, stretching my limbs out into liquid-filled spaces as my heart beat its first beats. An umbilical cord attached to my belly wound its way to Mama's placenta, where the food she ate entered my body the way air enters a diver's body through a gas tank.

A few months later, I plumped out and she began to tilt forward with my weight as I turned and kicked the inside wall of her belly. She stroked the perimeter of her globe to feel my foot. The war was ending, the U.S. was retreating, and another war was beginning. Mama breathed in yellow as the sun made her dress stick to her skin and she tried not to notice the communist soldiers patrolling the streets. Military helicopters twirled in the sky. Her hand was holding my two-year-old brother's hand as she walked and wondered about our "baba" (papa), "He was supposed to report to the new regime for ten days, but where is he now? Dead or alive?"

The following year, Mama's body forced me out. For the next couple of months, she nourished me at her breasts and occasionally I drifted off to sleep while the warm milk flowed through my body. Soon Mama went to work selling soybean juice on the street in front of a hospital while "Por por" (Maternal Grandma) watched my brother and me. Por-por carried me on her back in a cloth pouch tied around her shoulders and waist and I bounced up and down, knocking out some of her teeth.

An aunt said to Mama, "Why don't you sell your baby? You don't have food to eat." My brother, not understanding that it was a sick joke, replied, "No, don't sell my sister! Look, there are lots of cockroaches for us to eat!"

Cockroaches

The dark room was sparsely lit by a blue moon as I sat on the floor. I was a year old. Cockroaches scurried like mice along the walls. I was exploring the world with my senses. My fingers pressed against the dimensions of dirt on the floor, memorizing its texture. The air smelled wide and empty like the room. I squeezed a cockroach between my fingers. It popped. Hard on the outside and soft on the inside. My fingers were wet with its juices and wiggling body parts. My brother walked into the room and "eeeewwwwed" in disgust. It was an interesting world.

Hoang Lien Son Re-education Camp

Baba was a military captain in the ministry of law for the Republic of Vietnam. The Vietcong communists wanted to "re-educate" him.

On June 5, 1975, Baba reported to the Vietcong. Mama lost all contact with Baba for one year, then she was able to find out where they had taken him.

If Baba worked hard in the labor camp, every one or two years they let him read the letters Mama sent. Before he could read them, the letters were inspected by the Vietcong—they were not to be criticized in the letters.

Baba and about one thousand other prisoners worked in a forest in North Vietnam. They built a house for themselves with bamboo that they gathered in the forest. All the prisoners lived in this house and each one slept in a space about the length of his body. Every day, seven days a week, the prisoners dug holes, chopped bamboo and trees, built houses, and cooked for the Vietcong. In cold, windy weather, they walked barefoot up the mountains to find bamboo, trudging miles from mountain to mountain until their feet were bleeding and the soles were pink, red, and swollen, the exposed flesh scraping against rocks and branches. Due to the difficulty of finding the bamboo sticks, the weight of the sticks, and the weak, emaciated state of the prisoners, each one of them was usually only able to carry one bamboo back to camp each day.

They had no rest. Baba, like the other prisoners, wasn't given any meat or rice to eat. They gave him two meals a day, one in the afternoon and one at night. One meal would consist of fifty corn kernels, and Baba counted as he held each one between his thumb and index finger, slowly placing it on his tongue, savoring each bite. The meals alternated between corn kernels and small pieces of yucca root.

The prisoners were always hungry, always thinking about food, but after eating they felt even more hungry. At night, they chewed in their sleep and dreamt of eating.

One day, Baba fell down a mountain that was about three stories high because he was too tired and his feet collapsed under his own weight. He rolled down and lay there at the bottom like a sack of rice. His foot was injured and he couldn't walk. For a week, Baba wrapped his foot in heated lemon leaves and salt. He got better and continued to work.

If prisoners didn't follow the rules, they were forced to work more hours, deprived of food, beaten, tortured, put in isolation, or sentenced to death, depending on the seriousness of the offense. The Vietcong said to Baba and the other prisoners, "We don't need a bullet to kill you, 'cause you are not worth a bullet. We'll let you live like this to die day by day. You have to work for us, then you die."

Baba couldn't think about Mama, Brother, or me. If he did, he couldn't survive. He would break down. He would want to kill the people keeping him in prison or kill himself. He didn't think about anything at all. He told himself, "Don't feel, don't think, just survive."

Every couple of months, the prisoners were given weed to smoke.

When someone was put in re-education camp, there was no sentence; you could stay your whole life. They released you when they wanted to.

The Boat

It was October 21, 1978. The ethnic Chinese faced increasing discrimination and were not given any food or clothing. The U.S. gave asylum to those who worked for American companies and whose lives were at risk. Mama fit into both categories: she worked for an American company, and she was ethnically Chinese. She packed a change of clothes for my brother and me and we boarded a three-decked freight boat along with over twenty-five hundred other people fleeing the country. Mama's adoptive parents were stuck in Saigon because they had no papers to prove their relationship to her.

For three and a half months, the crowded boat was our home. We ate the little bits of food given to us in cans. People got sick and many died. When someone died due to sickness or rolled off a higher deck while asleep and died, they were wrapped in a blanket and thrown into the sea while someone said a Buddhist chant, "Nam mor ar may tor fat..."

I broke out into pimples, was continuously sick and coughing. Mama thought about our future and she cried. I was always crying and made Mama want to jump into the sea.

The boat was dirty, the floor we slept on was filthy, we were covered in grime. Mama cleaned my brother and me with a washcloth soaked in seawater.

We got to Singapore. Singapore didn't want to take us, Indonesia didn't want to take us. They gave us food on the boat and then we had to leave. The boat got to Malaysia. The Red Cross gave us food and let the boat stay in its waters for a while. We were given a spray for our hair to get rid of the fleas. We wrapped our heads in towels while we waited for the chemical to do its job and we washed it off with seawater. Malaysia let us enter the country to fly to the U.S.

On February 10, 1979, Mama, Brother, and I arrived in Los Angeles, California.

Snapshots of Early Childhood

When I was three years old, I was still drinking from a bottle and sucking my index finger. Mama was praying to Buddha and gave up eating beef in the hopes that it would contribute to our reunion with Baba.

In Saigon, Mama had worked for ten years as a telephone operator in an American trading company, so she knew some English. Mama studied data entry for eight months and got a job at Bank of America. She worked nights for a year, and I remember waking up crying to Grandma.

I continued sucking my finger in kindergarten until Uncle put chili pepper on my finger to get me to stop.

Mama, Brother, Grandma, and I lived with aunt, uncle, and their four sons in a faded yellow house on Allen Avenue in Pasadena until they moved to Missouri and we rented an apartment a couple of streets over on Parkwood. Shortly after that, Mama, Brother, Grandma, and I moved to a small house on Oak Avenue. The house was divided into two parts, and our neighbor Joe had two cats, Shadow, a black and white cat, and Snowy, a white cat with one blue eye and one yellow eye. Snowy's tail had been cut off by a kid and he always ran away from us. At that house, I met my first love—the garden.

Life was grass, bugs, flowers, and trees. I could eat bananas all day and climb the avocado tree or the plum tree, which was alternately full of flowers and fruits and naked, its branches clawing the sky. I would pick a plum, tear its skin with my teeth, and let its juice and flesh flood my mouth. I loved the fig tree, loved the fruits that bloodied the ground, loved sinking my teeth into the red, seedy meat.

The grass was great for flips, cartwheels and fights with my brother. My sky was green. I would track down butterflies and follow them around. I developed a hobby of catching butterflies by their wings, but I never kept any of them.

I was collecting spiders and would go around the garden, looking under leaves, in the cracks of the walls, under the rusting table, in corners, anywhere I could find a spider and put it in a jar. I had ten different spiders in a jar spinning ten different kinds of webs.

My brother and I would make villages out of branches and leaves from the avocado tree, dig up a trail around it, and pour water into the winding trench to make a stream.

I loved bananas so much. I was nine years old when I heard that Baba was coming. Baba was finally coming home! I always wanted a baba; the other kids had one, but I didn't. I was thinking, "What should I give him? It should be something really special." I decided to bring him a banana.

Mama got us ready and we drove to the airport in our yellow Datsun. I was holding the yellow banana and while I rode in the car, I felt something changing; I felt myself changing. Someone was coming to live with us. I thought about what I'd longed for for so long—a papa like the ones who picked up my friends from school. The ones with the faces that lit up when they saw my friends, the ones who hugged and smiled. A papa that swooped up his little daughter as if he held the world in his hands.

We waited at the airport and Baba got off the plane. I saw him and I started to cry; I cried and cried because I was scared. I saw my baba for the first time and I was scared that he'd be living with us. He was like an Egyptian cat: skinny, foraging, stern. He was impenetrable. He didn't smile; he didn't run up to swoop me into his arms. He was a stranger coming to live with us. I kept the banana, I kept crying in the car on our way home. Mama said, "See, your daughter is so glad to see you, she can't stop crying." I ate the banana.

My First Dinner with Baba

It was my first dinner with Baba after we picked him up from the airport. Grandma, Mama, Brother were there. We were sitting down for our first dinner together in nine years. We had rice, mixed vegetables and meat dishes, a typical Chinese dinner. Everyone had a pair of chopsticks. My brother and I had to "call" everyone before we could eat. "Ah Maa (paternal grandma) sik fan (eat meal), Ah Ba (papa) sik fan, Ah Ma (mama) sik fan." Before anyone could touch the food, we waited for Grandma to eat first. We all picked up our chopsticks, ready to eat. I held my chopsticks and Baba started to yell at me. I was scared; I was confused. He said that I couldn't use my left hand anymore; otherwise, he would punish me, and that I was bad because I was using my left hand. He said he wouldn't love me anymore if I did. His screaming paralyzed me; no one had ever screamed at me like that before. I began to cry. I didn't know how to use my right hand; I had never used it before for eating or writing and I didn't understand Baba. Mama had never punished me before for using my left hand. I did as he said because I thought he was going to beat me or kill me if I didn't. I knew my life was going to be different from then on. I wished he'd never come.

An Ax Stuck in My Memory

Life with Baba became very tense. I was scared to death of him. I didn't know when I was doing something wrong and would be yelled at and punished. He was always yelling at me for something. If I didn't put the bottle of sauce back at the exact spot where I found it, he would yell at and punish me. If I forgot to say, "good morning" or "good night" to him, he would yell at and punish me. I was becoming a paranoid child. Nevertheless, I decided to use my left hand. Learning to use my right hand was too difficult and I didn't think I was doing anything wrong. Still, I had no choice but to use my right hand to hold my chopsticks when we ate together. I hid behind doors and developed a knack for switching hands when Baba was walking into the room. When he walked near me, I nearly jumped in fear and impulsively moved away. I didn't talk to Baba because I hated him. I answered his questions using the fewest words possible, but I still seemed to always disappoint him.

Baba had a festering jealousy of my relationship with Mama. Was it because we loved each other? I never really understood why he didn't understand. Baba would curse Mama for being alone with me as if we were conspiring against him. So Mama didn't want to anger Baba and didn't stay alone with me anymore. I lost her.

One blinding yellow day, Mama was working in the garden and Baba was in the kitchen washing dishes. He insisted that I help him, so I did because I had no choice. What I really wanted to do was mess with dirt and plants with Mama. I went to help Mama after I washed the dishes, but apparently Baba was not satisfied and he was mad at me. When he started to yell and scream, I ran to my room like I always did and sat right in the middle of the floor to wait for things to calm down. They yelled at me to open the door. I didn't. Fear stiffened me up. I heard a loud crash—Baba was breaking down my bedroom door with an ax. He said he was going to kill me. I was screaming and crying. Mama was screaming and crying. She was shielding me as Baba lunged at me with the ax held above his head, saying he was going to kill me. The house was full of screams and the neighbor was tending her garden outside the window of the bedroom, quietly. Mama told Baba he would have to kill her first. He broke down every lock in the house with the ax and started to beat himself against the floor. We were destroyed.

A Knife

I was sitting on the floor behind the leaves of a potted plant, doing my homework. Baba was in the next room, in the kitchen. He was busy cooking; I could hear the clanging of dishes and pots and see the smoke that carried the aroma of food into the living room. Then a knife flew past my face, on the left side, missing it by an inch. Baba had seen me using my left hand and didn't like it. I thought that I could never forgive him. He could've killed me. Fear and anger became a constant reality. I lived with Baba, but pretended that he didn't exist. Otherwise, I couldn't have survived.

The Horse Stance

I was in elementary school. Baba had promised me that he would take me to some kind of event. The day before the event, while in the car, I reminded Baba that he had promised to take me to school that evening.

He said, "Well, no, I'm not taking you."

I asked pleadingly, "But why?"

He replied, "I'm just not taking you."

I was upset that Baba broke his promise and I had been looking forward to going. We got to our driveway and I got out to push open the gate so that the car could go in. I pushed the gate a bit harder than usual and Baba got mad at me for showing anger toward him. So I had to "chol houng hay" which literally means "sit in the air" also known as "the horse stance," a kind of Chinese punishment. My back had to be straight and not leaning against anything, I had to hold my ears with my hands, and my thighs had to be parallel to the floor. I had to sit as if I was sitting on a chair, except there was no chair. Five minutes of doing this and I couldn't stand it anymore: my thighs tightened up and I felt like the house was falling down on me. Baba put a stick across my thighs as I was sweating and sitting in the air and said if the stick dropped, then he would hit me. No one in the house could stop him; no one wanted to stop him. I was crying and Baba said that I had to stop crying or else he'd hit me. I felt like I was dying; I was shaking, sweating, crying, and my heart was broken. For two hours, Baba made me sit in the air with my back straight and a stick across my thighs. Finally, Grandma begged him to let me go. He let me go. I went to the bathroom and cried. I cried loudly, gasping for breath. Baba heard me crying and told me to stop. I couldn't stop, I couldn't stop it. He said that I had to go back to being punished. So, I went back to *chol houng hay*. It was one of the worst days of my life.

Ants

Toward winter, ants would come into the house and make trails along the bathtub. Before turning on the water to take a bath, I took each ant, one by one, out of the tub. The process was slow and usually took over half an hour. Once in a while, I would slightly squish one by accident. It would still be alive, just a bit twisted, and I would gently move it with my fingertip to straighten out its body and let it go. Some ants would get stuck in droplets of water and begin to drown; some would have drowned already. I took them out of the tub. The ones that were still alive were wet and couldn't move. I soaked up the water with a tissue, dried out the ant, and it would pitter-patter away. Sometimes I killed an ant, unintentionally, because I picked it up too quickly or with too much strength, and it would be crushed. I hated it when this happened, but it was inevitable.

Parakeets

Mama bought Brother and me two parakeets. One was yellow like the sun and one was blue like the sky. I was so excited; we put them in a cage and hung the cage up on a branch of the lemon tree. I stuck my fingers between the thin wires to try to rub my fingertip along the parakeets' feathers. We put a small cup of water and a cup of birdseed into the cage.

Two days later, I came home from school and the birdcage was empty! I cried and cried. My beautiful parakeets were gone! Grandma said that she let them go; she said that living things should not be kept in cages. The next day, I saw one of the parakeets in the lemon tree, fluttering in the leaves. I understood.

Grandma

The house was always filled with the smell of incense and the walls were brown with the smoke of incense. Grandma set up a shrine where she put a statue of Buddha, various other Buddhist figurines, and pictures of ancestors. I woke up in the morning to Grandma chanting and saw the gray smoke seep into the cracks of my bedroom door. Every once in a while, she banged a black metal gong shaped like a bowl with her red wooden stick. It was a ritual when she prayed: she would take out her mat and spread it on the floor before the altar, put on her dark brown robe, get her beaded necklace that she rotated around her fingers, ceremoniously light the incense, and stick it into a bowl of ash. She was not to be disturbed for the next half hour, or until she was done. She meditated three times a day: once in the morning, once in the afternoon, and once before bed.

Red

Baba refused to wear anything that was the color red. He said that it was a good thing that Mama's car wasn't red; otherwise, he would've repainted it. He said he hated red because he said it was the color of communism.

Chicks

I was about seven years old. It was a hot day and I was hurrying back from school to play with the baby chicks Mama bought us. There were about ten of them. They were little balls of yellow fluff. Some of the chicks were yellow like the color of a banana, some of them were yellow like the color of Mama's car, some were yellow like the color of a faded sweater. We would let them run around the banana trees and flowers. When I picked one up in my hand, I could feel that it was soft and light. I came home from school and opened the door to the laundry room that was attached to the house. The chicks were in a box on the floor. I looked into the box and there were ants crawling everywhere. A few of the chicks were already dead. Most of them were moving around, the ants walking in and out of their bodies and guts, eating them alive. Some ants were walking through a chick's head. The chick was standing with its eyes open, taking a few steps here and there. Blood was dripping from holes in the chick's body. There was nowhere it could go, nothing it could do but let itself be eaten alive. I screamed and screamed. I found a chick that was still salvageable, that was mildly injured, and took it out. It was the only one that survived for a while.

Dripping

I was about eleven years old. I was alone at home with Baba; I dreaded this moment. I planned to do whatever I could to avoid being punished. I sat quietly at the dinner table doing my homework.

Baba asked me, "Do you hear that?"

I began to curl. "Hear what?" I asked.

"Do you hear it?"

I tried my best to invoke my strongest listening abilities to hear "it." "No. Sorry."

"The water is dripping. Why didn't you hear it and fix it?" he asked.

I said, "I just didn't hear it."

He punished me—I had to sit in the air with no chair.

Grandma's Sofa

There was a specific sofa that was known as Grandma's sofa. We had two sofas in the house and one of them belonged to Grandma. She sat there when she sipped her tea and when she methodically combed her long, gray and white hair, twisted it into a bun at the back of her head, and clipped it tight. She decorated her hair and kept it in immaculate place with clips and pins. She held the end of a bobby pin between her teeth as she moved her hair into place with her fingers, looking into the small, round mirror on the coffee table.

Trip to Saigon

In the summer of 1995, I went back to Vietnam. I really wanted to go visit my maternal grandma, Por-por. I was teaching English in Pusan, South Korea at the time and had a break—my perfect opportunity. Vietnam was just next door. Conditions in Vietnam were still corrupt and chaotic, so my parents were nervous at the thought of me going there, but I had my mind set and couldn't be deterred.

When we left Vietnam in 1978, my grandparents on Mama's side were stranded. In subsequent years, Mama saved money to send to her parents so that they could build a comfortable place to live in. Por-por's son, whom she had adopted the way she had adopted Mama, was a big gambler and he soon gambled the house away. So, the son would send letters to Mama blackmailing her, writing that if she didn't send him money, then he would take their parents out into the woods and chop off their legs. "Gong-gong" (Paternal Grandpa) died shortly afterward from what we suspect was a heart attack from hearing about this.

In Saigon, I stayed with some distant relatives. I was intensely nervous about going back to Vietnam; every emotion was magnified. In the city, the popular form of transportation was the motorcycle, and I rode along with some cousins. The air was thick with exhaust; a greasy film covered my face when I went outside. I could see the smelly black-and-white clouds of polluted air when I rode on the motorcycle.

Apartments were fragilely built and looked as if a strong wind could have blown them over into the sandy streets. Sheets covered openings in the walls. People sold food and knick-knacks on the street under the apartments. Conversations and engines filled my ears. A couple of small children, about seven years old, ran up to me with a bowl in their hands, begging for food and money. People were worried that the government would force them to leave their homes and move to the countryside. The party flag and the flag of Communist Vietnam still waved side by side, like brothers.

Por-por didn't know that I was coming. We couldn't tell her because of her son. A relative drove me to where she lived; a man stood outside the house as if guarding the entrance. I went inside and told her who I was, that I was "AhWai," and gave her a hug. I remembered Mama telling me that Por-por couldn't use her legs anymore. She was living in a grimy, closet-sized room with a small bed and just enough room for me to squeeze in. She took out some pictures of me that Mama had sent her at different points in my life, growing. We hugged each other for a long time, letting the wet emotion run down our faces. Finally, after seventeen years, we were able to see each other again. I left Vietnam happier and sadder.

Baba

When Baba was in Hoang Lien Son "Re-education" Camp, his fellow inmates died of hunger, sickness, beatings. If someone attempted to escape and was caught, they would get one year in solitary confinement or the death penalty. Some were bludgeoned to death in front of the other prisoners. Some prisoners were hung upside down from the ceiling and beaten as they swung, and if they screamed in pain they were beaten some more. As punishment, prisoners were tied up in excruciating positions, shackled, and placed in small boxes where their tied-up legs became gangrenous and had to be chopped off. Prisoners were punished for "reactionary statements," forced to work more hours and deprived of their small ration of food. Prisoners died during interrogation. There was a list of rules they had to memorize and follow.

Scars

Mama showed me the scars on her hands where her adoptive parents had beat her with a stick when they hung her from the ceiling when she didn't listen. The scars are a rise in the flesh where the new skin covers the broken skin, just like the scar I have on my left middle finger from when I grabbed a glass vase so hard that it shattered in my hand.

Mama looks at me in shock that I complain about my childhood. She loves her scars; she says that they were created out of love. Her reasoning is that her real parents abandoned her; at least her adoptive parents raised her.

How meaning changes when situation is put beside situation. My childhood: a horror to some, a blessing to others. One person's life: a horror to some, a blessing to others.

Bedtime Story

Mama used to tell us a bedtime story that somehow managed to make me fall asleep. Here it goes:

Once upon a time, two kids, a brother and a sister, lived with their mother in the woods. One day, while the kids were out, a witch came to the cottage and ate the mother. At night, the kids came home and knocked on the door, calling, "Mother, open the door!" The witch blew out all the candles and opened the door.

The kids asked, "Mother, why is it so dark? Can you light the lamps?"

The witch said, "My eyes are hurting and the lights will hurt them, besides it's late and it's time for bed."

They all slept together in one big bed. In the middle of the night, the brother heard a crackling sound. He asked, "Mother, what is that sound?"

"I'm eating some nuts."

"Can I have some?"

"No, it's late. Go to sleep." The boy, in bed, felt around with his hands for his sister. She wasn't there.

He realized that the mother or witch or whoever it was, was eating his sister, munching on her bones.

I don't remember the ending...

Acknowledgments

Thank you to the editors of the following journals, and thank you to my family and friends for all of your support and encouragement.

Year of the Hare first appeared in *Memoir Journal* in Spring/Summer 2009, Issue Volume 2, Number 1. *Year of the Hare* was republished online in *Big Bridge* (2013), archived by the LOCKSS system.

www.ingramcontent.com/pod-product-compliance
Lightning Source LLC
LaVergne TN
LVHW050950080826
845145LV00004B/1456

* 9 7 8 0 9 8 5 3 1 5 1 5 3 *